I0002213

I. Introduction
    A. Definition of digital marketing
    B. Importance of digital marketing in today's world
    C. Objectives of the book

II. Understanding the target audience
    A. Identifying the target audience
    B. Segmentation of target audience
    C. Understanding the buyer's journey

III. Building a Strong Online Presence
    A. Developing a website
    B. Utilizing social media platforms
    C. Establishing a brand image

IV. Search Engine Optimization (SEO)
    A. Definition of SEO
    B. Keyword research
    C. On-page and off-page optimization
    D. Measuring the success of SEO efforts

V. Content Marketing
    A. Definition of content marketing
    B. Types of content
    C. Content creation and distribution
    D. Measuring the success of content marketing

VI. Email Marketing
    A. Definition of email marketing
    B. Building an email list
    C. Creating email campaigns

D. Measuring the success of email marketing

VII. Paid Advertising
    A. Introduction to paid advertising
    B. Pay-per-click (PPC) advertising
    C. Social media advertising
    D. Display advertising
    E. Measuring the success of paid advertising

VIII. Mobile Marketing
    A. Definition of mobile marketing
    B. Importance of mobile optimization
    C. Mobile apps and mobile-friendly websites
    D. Measuring the success of mobile marketing

IX. Marketing Automation
    A. Definition of marketing automation
    B. Benefits of marketing automation
    C. Choosing the right marketing automation tools
    D. Measuring the success of marketing automation

X. Conclusion
    A. Recap of key takeaways
    B. Future trends in digital marketing
    C. Final thoughts

I. Introduction

Digital Marketing is a broad term that refers to advertising and promotion of products or services using digital technologies, including the internet, mobile devices, and other digital media. The objective of digital marketing is to reach a targeted audience through various digital channels such as search engines, social media, email, and websites, and convert them into customers. Digital marketing allows companies to measure the effectiveness of their campaigns and target their audience in real-time, leading to increased efficiency and cost-effectiveness compared to traditional marketing methods.

A. Definition of digital marketing

Digital Marketing is a marketing strategy that utilizes digital technologies, including the internet, mobile devices, and other digital media channels, to reach and engage with a target audience with the ultimate goal of promoting a product, service, or brand and converting the target audience into customers. This type of marketing allows for more precise targeting, real-time analytics, and greater overall efficiency and cost-effectiveness compared to traditional marketing methods.

B. Importance of digital marketing in today's world

Digital Marketing is becoming increasingly important in today's world as a growing number of consumers rely on digital channels to research, purchase and interact with businesses. Some of the key reasons why digital marketing is important include:

Reach: Digital marketing allows businesses to reach a larger and more targeted audience than traditional marketing methods.

Engagement: Digital marketing channels such as social media and email enable businesses to engage with their customers and build relationships.

Data and Analytics: Digital marketing provides businesses with real-time data and analytics to measure the effectiveness of their campaigns and make data-driven decisions.

Cost-effectiveness: Digital marketing is often more cost-effective than traditional marketing methods, allowing small businesses to compete with larger ones.

Adaptability: Digital marketing allows businesses to quickly adapt their campaigns in response to changes in consumer behavior and market conditions.

In summary, digital marketing is important for businesses of all sizes in today's digital-first world, as it provides a powerful and cost-effective way to reach and engage with customers, gain valuable insights, and drive business growth.

C. Objectives of the book

The objectives of a digital marketing book can vary depending on the author's perspective and target audience. However, some common objectives of digital marketing books include:

Providing an overview of digital marketing: The book may aim to provide an in-depth understanding of what digital marketing is, how it differs from traditional marketing, and its role in today's business landscape.

Teaching digital marketing techniques: The book may aim to teach readers the various digital marketing techniques and strategies that are currently being used, such as search engine optimization (SEO), pay-per-click advertising (PPC), social media marketing, email marketing, and content marketing.

Sharing best practices: The book may share best practices and case studies of successful digital marketing campaigns, providing readers with actionable insights they can apply to their own marketing efforts.

Discussing new and emerging trends: The book may aim to keep readers up to date on the latest digital marketing trends and technologies, such as artificial intelligence, machine learning, and voice search optimization.

Offering practical advice: The book may offer practical advice and guidelines to help readers create and execute successful digital marketing campaigns, including how to measure the success of their efforts.

Overall, the objectives of a digital marketing book will vary, but the goal is typically to provide readers with a comprehensive understanding of digital marketing, the techniques and strategies involved, and how they can be used to drive business growth and success.

II. Understanding the target audience

The target audience of a digital marketing book can vary depending on the author's intended audience, level of expertise, and specific topic being covered. Some common target audiences for digital marketing books include:

Marketing professionals: Digital marketing books can be targeted towards experienced marketing professionals looking to further their understanding of the subject and stay up-to-date with the latest trends and best practices.

Entrepreneurs and small business owners: Digital marketing books can be targeted towards entrepreneurs and small business owners who want to learn how to promote their products or services online and reach their target audience effectively.

Students and educators: Digital marketing books can be targeted towards students of marketing, advertising, or related fields, as well as educators who teach digital marketing.

Anyone interested in digital marketing: Digital marketing books can also be targeted towards a general audience of anyone who is interested in learning about digital marketing and how it can be used to promote a business or personal brand.

In determining the target audience, the author of the digital marketing book must consider the level of expertise of the readers, their specific needs and interests, and the type of information that is most relevant and valuable to them. This can help the author create content that is engaging, relevant, and actionable for the target audience.

A. Identifying the target audience

Identifying the target audience is a crucial step in digital marketing, as it allows marketers to tailor their marketing efforts and messages to the people who are most likely to be interested in their products or services. Some common methods for identifying the target audience include:

Demographic analysis: This involves analyzing data on age, gender, income, education level, and other demographic characteristics to identify patterns and target specific groups of consumers.

Psychographic analysis: This involves examining consumers' values, interests, and lifestyle habits to better understand their motivations and decision-making processes.

Behavioral analysis: This involves analyzing data on how consumers interact with products and services, including purchase history, website behavior, and other engagement metrics.

Customer surveys and feedback: This involves collecting direct feedback from customers through surveys, focus groups, and other feedback mechanisms to gain a deeper understanding of their needs and preferences.

Competitor analysis: This involves analyzing the target audience of a company's competitors to understand who they are targeting and why.

By combining these methods and gathering data from multiple sources, businesses can build a detailed picture of their target audience, including who they are, what they want, and how they behave. This information can then be used to inform the development of a digital marketing strategy that is tailored to the specific needs and interests of the target audience.

B. Segmentation of target audience

Segmenting the target audience refers to the process of dividing a larger audience into smaller, more specific groups based on shared characteristics or behaviors. This allows businesses to tailor their marketing efforts to the specific needs and preferences of each group, resulting in more effective and efficient marketing.

There are several ways to segment a target audience, including:

Demographic segmentation: This involves dividing the target audience based on demographic characteristics such as age, gender, income, education level, and geographic location.

Psychographic segmentation: This involves dividing the target audience based on values, personality, lifestyle, and interests.

Behavioral segmentation: This involves dividing the target audience based on their behaviors, such as purchase history, product usage, and brand loyalty.

Geographic segmentation: This involves dividing the target audience based on their geographic location, such as country, region, city, or neighborhood.

Technographic segmentation: This involves dividing the target audience based on their technology usage and preferences, such as the devices they use, the apps they have installed, and their online habits.

By segmenting the target audience, businesses can create more effective and relevant marketing campaigns, better understand their customers, and ultimately drive more sales and customer loyalty.

C. Understanding the buyer's journey

The buyer's journey refers to the process that a consumer goes through in order to make a purchase decision, from awareness of a need or problem to evaluation of solutions and finally to the purchase decision itself. Understanding the buyer's journey is crucial for businesses in order to develop effective digital marketing strategies that can influence the consumer at each stage of the journey.

The buyer's journey typically consists of three stages:

Awareness: In this stage, the consumer becomes aware of a need or problem and begins to gather information about potential solutions.

Consideration: In this stage, the consumer evaluates the options and narrows down the choices to a smaller group of potential solutions.

Decision: In this stage, the consumer makes a final decision and chooses a solution to purchase.

At each stage of the buyer's journey, the consumer has different needs and is looking for different types of information. By understanding the buyer's journey, businesses can create marketing messages that are tailored to each stage, providing the consumer with the information they need at the right time to move them towards a purchase decision.

By aligning their marketing efforts with the buyer's journey, businesses can create more effective and efficient marketing campaigns that ultimately lead to increased sales and customer loyalty.

III. Building a Strong Online Presence

Building a strong online presence is a critical aspect of digital marketing and helps businesses establish their brand, reach new customers, and build relationships with existing ones. There are several key elements to building a strong online presence, including:

Website: A well-designed website is the foundation of a strong online presence and provides a platform for businesses to showcase their products and services, provide information, and engage with customers.

Search Engine Optimization (SEO): SEO is the process of optimizing a website to improve its visibility and ranking in search engines like Google. This includes optimizing the website's content, structure, and technical elements to make it more appealing to search engines and users.

Social Media: Social media platforms like Facebook, Instagram, and Twitter provide businesses with an opportunity to connect with customers, share content, and build brand awareness.

Content Marketing: Content marketing involves creating and sharing valuable, relevant, and engaging content to attract and retain customers and ultimately drive profitable customer action.

Email Marketing: Email marketing is a cost-effective way for businesses to reach and engage with customers and build relationships. This includes sending newsletters, promotional emails, and other types of communications to subscribers.

Online Advertising: Online advertising provides businesses with the opportunity to reach specific target audiences with targeted messages. This includes paid search advertising, display advertising, and social media advertising.

By focusing on these key elements, businesses can build a strong online presence that helps them reach their target audience, increase brand awareness, and drive sales.

A. Developing a website

Developing a website is a critical step in building a strong online presence and creating a platform for businesses to engage with customers, showcase products and services, and provide information. Here are several key steps involved in developing a website:

Define the website's purpose: Before starting the development process, it's important to determine what the website will be used for and what it should achieve.

Choose a domain name: A domain name is the address of a website, such as www.example.com. Choosing the right domain name is important as it helps establish the website's identity and makes it easier for customers to find the website.

Select a platform: There are several website platforms available, including WordPress, Wix, Shopify, and others. Choosing the right platform depends on the website's purpose, budget, and technical expertise.

Design the website: This involves creating a layout, choosing colors and fonts, and adding images and other elements to create a visually appealing website.

Add content: This includes adding text, images, videos, and other types of content to the website to provide information and engage with customers.

Optimize for search engines: This involves optimizing the website's content, structure, and technical elements to improve its visibility and ranking in search engines like Google.

Test the website: Before launching the website, it's important to test it to ensure it's functioning properly and all elements are working as intended.

Launch the website: Once the website is complete and tested, it's ready to be launched and made available to the public.

By following these steps, businesses can develop a website that helps them reach their target audience, increase brand awareness, and drive sales.

B. Utilizing social media platforms

Utilizing social media platforms is an important aspect of digital marketing as it provides businesses with an opportunity to reach and engage with customers, build brand awareness, and drive sales. Here are several key steps for utilizing social media platforms effectively:

Choose the right platforms: Not all social media platforms are right for every business. It's important to choose platforms where the target audience is active and engage with the business's content.

Establish a consistent brand image: Social media profiles should reflect the business's brand image and values, including the use of similar logos, colors, and images.

Create and share valuable content: Social media is a great platform for sharing valuable, relevant, and engaging content with customers, including blog posts, infographics, and videos.

Engage with followers: Responding to comments and messages from followers helps build relationships with customers and establishes the business as an expert in its field.

Monitor metrics: Use metrics to track the performance of social media campaigns and make data-driven decisions about what's working and what's not.

Advertise on social media: Utilizing paid advertising options on social media platforms can help businesses reach specific target audiences and drive sales.

By following these steps, businesses can effectively utilize social media platforms to reach and engage with customers, build brand awareness, and drive sales.

C. Establishing a brand image

Establishing a strong brand image is a critical aspect of digital marketing, as it helps businesses differentiate themselves from competitors and establish a unique identity in the marketplace. Here are several key steps for establishing a brand image:

Define your brand: Define the values, mission, and personality of the brand to create a consistent message and image.

Develop a visual identity: This includes creating a logo, color scheme, and other visual elements that reflect the brand's image and values.

Create brand guidelines: Establish guidelines for how the brand should be represented, including the use of logos, colors, and messaging, to ensure consistency across all channels.

Consistently communicate the brand: Consistently communicate the brand message and image through all marketing channels, including the website, social media, and advertising.

Engage with customers: Building relationships with customers helps establish the brand as a trusted and reliable source of information and products.

Monitor and adjust: Continuously monitor the brand's performance and adjust the brand image and message as needed to ensure it remains relevant and appealing to customers.

By following these steps, businesses can establish a strong brand image that helps them differentiate themselves from competitors, build customer trust and loyalty, and drive sales.

IV. Search Engine Optimization (SEO)

Search Engine Optimization (SEO) is the process of optimizing a website to improve its visibility and ranking in search engines like Google. The goal of SEO is to increase organic (non-paid) traffic to a website by making it more visible to users when they search for relevant keywords. Here are several key steps for effective SEO:

Conduct keyword research: Identify keywords and phrases that are relevant to the business and target audience and that have high search volume.

Optimize website content: Optimize website content, including page titles, meta descriptions, and header tags, to include relevant keywords and make it more visible to search engines.

Improve website structure: Ensure the website has a clear and logical structure, including a well-defined hierarchy and navigation, to make it easy for users and search engines to find content.

Build high-quality links: High-quality links from other relevant websites to the business's website can help improve the website's visibility and ranking in search engines.

Monitor and adjust: Continuously monitor the website's performance, using tools like Google Analytics, and adjust the SEO strategy as needed to improve visibility and ranking.

By following these steps, businesses can effectively improve their SEO and increase their organic traffic, making it easier for customers to find their website and products.

A. Definition of SEO

Search Engine Optimization (SEO) is the process of optimizing a website to rank higher in search engines like Google, with the goal of increasing organic (non-paid) traffic. This includes improving the technical and content aspects of a website to make it more visible and appealing to both search engines and users. SEO involves keyword research, content optimization, link building, and website structure optimization, among other tactics, to help websites rank higher in search results pages for relevant keywords and phrases. The ultimate goal of SEO is to improve the visibility and ranking of a website, making it easier for users to find the website and its products or services.

B. Keyword research

Keyword research is a crucial aspect of search engine optimization (SEO), as it helps determine the keywords and phrases that potential customers use to search for products or services related to a business. Keyword research helps businesses understand the language and terms their target audience is using to find what they're looking for, and helps guide the development of content that is optimized for these keywords. Here are several steps for effective keyword research:

Identify the target audience: Determine who the target audience is and what they're searching for.

Brainstorm a list of keywords: Start with a broad list of keywords and phrases related to the business and target audience, including both short- and long-tail keywords.

Use keyword research tools: Use keyword research tools, such as Google Keyword Planner, to gather data on keyword popularity, search volume, and competition.

Analyze search results: Look at the search results for the keywords to see what types of content are ranking and what type of competition exists.

Prioritize keywords: Prioritize keywords based on their relevance, search volume, and competition level.

By conducting keyword research, businesses can determine the keywords and phrases their target audience is using, and use this information to optimize their website content, improve their visibility in search results, and drive more organic traffic to their site.

C. On-page and off-page optimization

On-page optimization and off-page optimization are two critical components of search engine optimization (SEO).

On-page optimization refers to the optimization of individual web pages to rank higher in search engines. This includes optimizing website content and structure, including page titles, meta descriptions, header tags, and the website's overall structure, to make it more visible and appealing to search engines and users.

Off-page optimization refers to the optimization of elements outside of the website, such as building high-quality links from other relevant websites, to improve the website's visibility and ranking in search engines. The quality and quantity of links from other sites to a website is a key factor in determining a website's visibility and ranking in search results.

Both on-page and off-page optimization are important for achieving a strong online presence and improving search engine visibility. Businesses should focus on both types of optimization to maximize their visibility in search results, drive more organic traffic to their website, and improve their search engine rankings.

D. Measuring the success of SEO efforts

Measuring the success of SEO efforts is important to determine whether the strategies used are effective and to make data-driven decisions for future optimization. Here are several metrics that can be used to measure the success of SEO efforts:

Organic Traffic: The number of visitors coming to a website from search engines through non-paid search results. This is a key indicator of how well a website is ranking in search results and how effectively it's attracting organic traffic.

Keyword Rankings: The position a website is ranking for specific keywords in search engine results pages (SERPs). Tracking keyword rankings helps determine how well a website is ranking for important keywords and can indicate areas for improvement.

Bounce Rate: The percentage of visitors who leave a website after only visiting one page. A high bounce rate may indicate that the website content is not relevant or engaging to visitors.

Time on Site: The average amount of time visitors spend on a website. A high time on site can indicate that the website content is engaging and relevant to visitors.

Conversion Rates: The percentage of visitors who take a desired action, such as making a purchase or filling out a form. Increased conversion rates indicate that a website is effectively converting visitors into customers.

By regularly monitoring and analyzing these metrics, businesses can measure the success of their SEO efforts, identify areas for improvement, and make data-driven decisions for future optimization.

V. Content Marketing

Content marketing is a strategic marketing approach focused on creating and sharing valuable, relevant, and consistent content to attract and retain a clearly defined target audience and ultimately drive profitable customer action. The goal of content marketing is to build a strong relationship with the target audience by providing valuable information that helps solve their problems or meet their needs, rather than directly promoting a product or service.

Types of content used in content marketing can include blog posts, articles, infographics, videos, podcasts, e-books, and more. The content is distributed through various channels such as a company's website, social media platforms, email marketing, and other online channels.

Effective content marketing requires a deep understanding of the target audience and their needs, as well as a well-defined content strategy that outlines the types of content to be produced, the channels used to distribute the content, and the goals and objectives of the content marketing efforts. By creating valuable content and building a strong relationship with the target audience, businesses can drive more website traffic, generate leads, and ultimately increase sales.

A. Definition of content marketing

Content marketing is a strategic marketing approach focused on creating and sharing valuable, relevant, and consistent content with the purpose of attracting and retaining a clearly defined target audience and ultimately driving profitable customer action. It involves creating and distributing valuable information, such as articles, videos, infographics, blog posts, and more, to educate and engage the target audience and build trust and credibility with them.

The goal of content marketing is to establish a relationship with the target audience and provide them with information they find useful and relevant, rather than directly promoting a product or service. By consistently providing valuable content, businesses can attract more website traffic, generate leads, and increase sales over time.

B. Types of content

There are many types of content that can be used in a content marketing strategy. Here are some of the most common types of content:

Blog Posts: Informative articles or posts that provide information and insights on a specific topic or industry.

Videos: Engaging and informative videos that can be used to educate, entertain, or demonstrate a product or service.

Infographics: Visually appealing graphics that present information and data in a clear and easy-to-understand format.

E-books: Long-form content pieces that provide in-depth information on a specific topic.

Case Studies: Detailed reports that showcase the results and impact of a product or service for a specific customer or industry.

White Papers: In-depth research-based reports that provide insights and solutions on a specific topic or issue.

Podcasts: Audio content that can be used to educate or entertain the target audience on a specific topic.

Social Media Posts: Short and engaging posts that can be used to promote content, build brand awareness, and engage with the target audience on social media platforms.

Webinars: Live or pre-recorded events that provide education and insights on a specific topic.

By using a combination of these types of content, businesses can reach and engage their target audience and provide valuable information that helps them solve their problems or meet their needs.

C. Content creation and distribution

Content creation is the process of developing valuable and relevant content that is tailored to meet the needs and interests of a target audience. This can include writing blog posts, creating videos, designing infographics, and more. The content should be well-researched, informative, and engaging, and it should align with the overall goals and objectives of the content marketing strategy.

Once the content is created, it must be distributed effectively to reach the target audience. There are several channels that can be used to distribute content, including:

Company website: The company's own website is a key channel for distributing content, as it provides a platform to showcase the brand's expertise and authority in its industry.

Social media platforms: Popular social media platforms like Facebook, Twitter, LinkedIn, and Instagram can be used to share content and engage with the target audience.

Email marketing: Email newsletters and promotional campaigns can be used to deliver content directly to the target audience's inbox.

Influencer marketing: Partnering with influencers in the same industry can help reach a wider audience and increase the visibility of the content.

Paid advertising: Paid advertising, such as Google AdWords or Facebook Ads, can be used to drive traffic to the content and reach a larger audience.

By using a combination of these channels, businesses can effectively distribute their content and reach a large and engaged audience. However, it's important to track the results of these efforts and make adjustments as needed to ensure the best possible return on investment.

D. Measuring the success of content marketing

Measuring the success of a content marketing strategy is important to ensure that the effort and resources invested are delivering the desired results. There are several metrics that can be used to measure the success of a content marketing strategy, including:

Traffic: The number of visitors to the website or landing page where the content is hosted.

Engagement: The level of engagement with the content, such as the number of comments, shares, and likes on social media.

Lead Generation: The number of leads generated from the content, such as contact form submissions, newsletter sign-ups, or downloads of gated content.

Conversion Rates: The percentage of visitors who take a desired action, such as making a purchase or filling out a form.

ROI: The return on investment for the content marketing effort, including the cost of content creation, distribution, and promotion.

By regularly monitoring these metrics, businesses can assess the effectiveness of their content marketing efforts and make changes as needed to improve their results. Additionally, tracking the results of individual pieces of content can help businesses identify what types of content resonates best with their target audience and optimize their content marketing strategy accordingly.

VI. Email Marketing

Email marketing is a digital marketing strategy that involves sending promotional or informative messages directly to a target audience through email. It is an effective way to reach potential and existing customers, build relationships, and drive conversions.

To get started with email marketing, businesses need to build a list of subscribers who have opted-in to receive emails from the company. This can be done through sign-ups on the company website, lead magnets, or other incentives.

Once the email list is established, businesses can create and send emails that are tailored to the specific interests and needs of the target audience. Effective email marketing campaigns should be well-designed, relevant, and valuable to the recipient.

There are several key components of a successful email marketing campaign, including:

Segmentation: The process of dividing the email list into smaller groups based on specific criteria, such as demographics, interests, or behavior.

Personalization: Customizing the content and messaging of the emails to make them more relevant and appealing to the recipient.

Testing: Regularly testing different elements of the email campaigns, such as subject lines, call-to-action, and design, to determine what works best and make improvements.

Tracking: Regularly tracking the results of the email marketing efforts, such as open rates, click-through rates, and conversions, to assess the effectiveness of the campaigns and make improvements as needed.

By using email marketing effectively, businesses can increase their reach, build stronger relationships with their target audience, and drive conversions and sales.

A. Definition of email marketing

Email marketing is a digital marketing strategy that involves sending promotional or informational messages directly to a target audience through email. The goal of email marketing is to build relationships with potential and existing customers, promote products or services, and drive conversions. Email marketing allows businesses to reach a large number of people in a cost-effective and targeted way. To be effective, email marketing campaigns should be well-designed, relevant, and valuable to the recipient. This typically involves segmenting the email list, personalizing the content and messaging, regularly testing and tracking the results, and making improvements as needed.

B. Building an email list

Building an email list is a crucial step in launching a successful email marketing campaign. A well-built email list provides businesses with a direct line of communication to their target audience and is a valuable asset for driving conversions and sales.

There are several ways to build an email list, including:

Website Sign-Ups: Adding a sign-up form to the company website and encouraging visitors to subscribe to the email list.

Lead Magnets: Offering a free resource, such as an e-book, webinar, or template, in exchange for an email address.

Content Upgrades: Adding a sign-up form to specific pieces of content, such as blog posts or landing pages, and offering a relevant resource in exchange for an email address.

Events and Networking: Collecting email addresses at events, trade shows, and networking events.

Purchase or Inquiry: Collecting email addresses from customers who make a purchase or inquiry about the company's products or services.

Once the email list is established, it is important to regularly maintain and grow the list by adding new subscribers and removing inactive or unengaged members. This helps ensure that the email list remains targeted and effective for driving conversions and sales.

C. Creating email campaigns

Creating email campaigns is a key part of a successful email marketing strategy. An effective email campaign should be well-designed, relevant, and valuable to the recipient.

To create a successful email campaign, businesses should follow these steps:

Define the goal: Determine what the email campaign is meant to achieve, such as building relationships, promoting a product, or driving conversions.

Identify the target audience: Segment the email list based on specific criteria, such as demographics, interests, or behavior, to make the content and messaging more relevant and appealing to the recipient.

Create the content: Write the content for the email, including the subject line, body copy, images, and call-to-action. Make sure the content is relevant, valuable, and tailored to the target audience.

Design the email: Choose an attractive and professional design that aligns with the company's brand and appeals to the target audience.

Test the email: Before sending the email campaign, test it thoroughly to ensure it is well-designed, properly formatted, and free of technical errors.

Launch the campaign: Send the email campaign to the target audience and track the results, such as open rates, click-through rates, and conversions.

Evaluate the results: After the campaign has been launched, analyze the results and make improvements as needed. Regularly testing and optimizing the email campaigns is a crucial part of a successful email marketing strategy.

By following these steps, businesses can create effective and engaging email campaigns that drive conversions and build strong relationships with their target audience.

D. Measuring the success of email marketing

Measuring the success of email marketing campaigns is essential for understanding the effectiveness of the efforts and making improvements.

The following metrics can be used to measure the success of email marketing:

Open Rate: The percentage of people who opened the email out of the total number of recipients.

Click-Through Rate (CTR): The percentage of people who clicked on a link within the email.

Conversion Rate: The percentage of people who took a desired action, such as making a purchase or filling out a form, after receiving the email.

Bounce Rate: The percentage of emails that were undeliverable and returned to the sender as undeliverable.

Spam Complaint Rate: The percentage of recipients who marked the email as spam.

Unsubscribe Rate: The percentage of recipients who opted out of future emails.

By tracking these metrics, businesses can determine the effectiveness of their email marketing efforts and make improvements as needed. For example, if the open rate is low, businesses can work on improving the subject line or preheader text to make the email more appealing. If the CTR is low, businesses can improve the content or design of the email to make it more engaging and relevant.

Measuring the success of email marketing efforts is an ongoing process, and businesses should regularly review and analyze their metrics to ensure their campaigns are effective and driving results.

VII. Paid Advertising

Paid advertising is a form of online marketing that involves paying for space on various platforms, such as search engines, social media, and websites, to promote a product or service. The goal of paid advertising is to drive traffic, generate leads, and increase conversions for a business.

There are several types of paid advertising, including:

Pay-Per-Click (PPC) Advertising: A form of advertising where businesses pay each time someone clicks on one of their ads.

Display Advertising: A form of advertising where businesses display an image or video ad on a website or other online platform.

Social Media Advertising: A form of advertising where businesses pay to promote their posts or ads on social media platforms, such as Facebook, Instagram, or Twitter.

Video Advertising: A form of advertising where businesses pay to display video ads on websites, social media platforms, or video streaming services.

Influencer Marketing: A form of advertising where businesses partner with influencers, or individuals with a large following on social media, to promote their product or service.

Each type of paid advertising has its own set of benefits and challenges, and businesses should carefully consider their target audience, budget, and goals when deciding which type of paid advertising to use.

By utilizing paid advertising, businesses can reach a large, targeted audience and achieve their marketing goals quickly and effectively. However, it's important to manage and monitor the advertising efforts to ensure they are effective and delivering a positive return on investment (ROI).

A. Introduction to paid advertising

Paid advertising is a type of online marketing that involves paying for space on various platforms, such as search engines, social media, websites, and more, to promote a product, service, or brand. The goal of paid advertising is to drive traffic, generate leads, and increase conversions for a business.

Paid advertising allows businesses to reach a large, targeted audience quickly and effectively, compared to traditional marketing methods. With the ability to target specific demographics, interests, behaviors, and more, paid advertising is a cost-effective way for businesses to reach their ideal customers.

There are various types of paid advertising, including Pay-Per-Click (PPC) advertising, display advertising, social media advertising, video advertising, and influencer marketing. Each type of paid advertising has its own set of benefits and challenges, and businesses should carefully consider their target audience, budget, and goals when deciding which type of paid advertising to use.

To maximize the effectiveness of paid advertising efforts, it's important to understand and analyze key performance metrics, such as click-through rates, conversion rates, and return on investment (ROI), to determine the success of the campaigns and make necessary adjustments.

Paid advertising can be a powerful tool for businesses looking to reach their marketing goals, but it should be used as part of a comprehensive marketing strategy and not relied upon as the sole means of promotion.

B. Pay-per-click (PPC) advertising

Pay-Per-Click (PPC) advertising is a form of online advertising where businesses pay each time someone clicks on one of their ads. PPC advertising is commonly used on search engines, such as Google and Bing, and on social media platforms, such as Facebook and Instagram.

With PPC advertising, businesses can bid on specific keywords or phrases related to their product or service, and their ad will be displayed when someone searches for those keywords. The bid amount, along with other factors, such as the relevance and quality of the ad, determines the placement of the ad in the search results.

PPC advertising allows businesses to reach a targeted audience who are actively searching for the products or services they offer. The cost of each click is determined by the bid amount and competition for the keywords, and businesses can set a daily budget for their campaigns to control spending.

To be successful with PPC advertising, businesses should conduct thorough keyword research, create compelling ad copy and landing pages, and constantly monitor and adjust their campaigns to ensure they are delivering a positive return on investment (ROI).

Overall, PPC advertising can be a cost-effective way for businesses to reach their ideal customers and achieve their marketing goals quickly. However, it's important to understand the mechanics of the platform and carefully manage and monitor campaigns to ensure they are effective and delivering a positive ROI.

C. Social media advertising

Social media advertising is a type of paid advertising that involves promoting products, services, or brands on social media platforms, such as Facebook, Instagram, Twitter, LinkedIn, and more.

Social media advertising allows businesses to reach a large, targeted audience quickly and effectively, based on demographic information, interests, behaviors, and more. With the ability to create visually engaging ads, businesses can grab the attention of potential customers and drive engagement.

There are various types of social media advertising, including image ads, video ads, carousel ads, and more, each with its own set of benefits and best practices.

To be successful with social media advertising, it's important to have a clear understanding of the target audience and create ads that resonate with them. This includes using eye-catching visuals, clear and concise messaging, and including a strong call to action.

Businesses can set a daily or lifetime budget for their campaigns and can also choose to pay per impression (CPM) or pay per click (CPC).

It's also important to regularly monitor and adjust campaigns based on performance metrics, such as click-through rate (CTR), conversion rate, and return on investment (ROI), to ensure that they are delivering a positive ROI.

Overall, social media advertising can be a powerful tool for businesses looking to reach their ideal customers and achieve their marketing goals. When used effectively, it can drive traffic, generate leads, and increase conversions for a business.

D. Display advertising

Display advertising is a form of online advertising that involves placing visual ads on websites and other digital platforms. The ads can be in various formats, including image ads, banner ads, video ads, and more.

Display advertising allows businesses to reach a large audience and target specific demographics, based on factors such as location, interests, and behaviors. The ads can be shown to potential customers as they browse websites, read articles, or use applications, and can be designed to be eye-catching and engaging.

To be successful with display advertising, businesses need to have a clear understanding of their target audience and create ads that resonate with them. This includes using visually appealing graphics, clear and concise messaging, and including a strong call to action.

Display advertising can be purchased through various ad networks, such as Google AdSense, and businesses can choose to pay per impression (CPM) or pay per click (CPC).

It's important to regularly monitor and adjust campaigns based on performance metrics, such as click-through rate (CTR), conversion rate, and return on investment (ROI), to ensure that they are delivering a positive ROI.

Overall, display advertising can be a cost-effective way for businesses to reach their ideal customers and achieve their marketing goals. When used effectively, it can drive traffic, generate leads, and increase conversions for a business.

E. Measuring the success of paid advertising

Measuring the success of paid advertising is an important aspect of any digital marketing campaign. It allows businesses to determine the return on investment (ROI) of their advertising efforts and make data-driven decisions about their marketing strategy.

Some of the key metrics for measuring the success of paid advertising include:

Cost per click (CPC): This metric measures the cost of each click on a paid ad. Lower CPCs indicate a more cost-effective campaign.

Click-through rate (CTR): CTR measures the number of clicks on an ad as a percentage of the total number of impressions. A high CTR indicates that the ad is resonating with its target audience.

Conversion rate: Conversion rate measures the percentage of visitors who take a desired action, such as making a purchase or filling out a form, after clicking on an ad.

Return on investment (ROI): ROI measures the profit made from a paid advertising campaign in comparison to the cost of the campaign. A positive ROI indicates that the campaign is delivering a positive return.

It's important to regularly track and analyze these metrics to determine the success of a paid advertising campaign and make informed decisions about how to optimize and improve future campaigns. This may involve adjusting ad copy, targeting, bidding strategies, and more, based on the performance data.

Overall, measuring the success of paid advertising is essential for ensuring that advertising efforts are delivering the desired results and helping businesses reach their marketing goals.

VIII. Mobile Marketing

Mobile marketing refers to marketing efforts that specifically target consumers through their mobile devices, such as smartphones and tablets. The goal of mobile marketing is to engage with customers on their mobile devices and reach them where they are most active.

Mobile marketing can take many forms, including SMS/MMS marketing, mobile apps, mobile search ads, mobile video ads, and more. The key to successful mobile marketing is to deliver relevant, valuable content to customers in a format that is easily accessible and engaging on their mobile devices.

Some common objectives of mobile marketing include increasing brand awareness, driving website traffic, and increasing sales or conversions. To achieve these objectives, marketers use tactics such as mobile-optimized email campaigns, targeted push notifications, and location-based promotions.

In today's world, where consumers spend increasing amounts of time on their mobile devices, mobile marketing has become an essential part of a comprehensive digital marketing strategy. By leveraging the unique features and capabilities of mobile devices, businesses can reach customers in new and innovative ways and build stronger relationships with them.

A. Definition of mobile marketing

Mobile marketing is a digital marketing strategy that uses mobile devices, such as smartphones and tablets, to reach and engage customers. The goal of mobile marketing is to deliver relevant and valuable content to customers through their mobile devices and build stronger relationships with them.

Mobile marketing can take many forms, including SMS/MMS marketing, mobile apps, mobile search ads, mobile video ads, and more. The key to successful mobile marketing is to understand the unique features and behaviors of mobile users and to deliver engaging, context-sensitive content to them through the right channels.

Overall, mobile marketing is a crucial component of a comprehensive digital marketing strategy, as it allows businesses to reach customers where they are most active and to build stronger relationships with them through personal, relevant interactions.

B. Importance of mobile optimization

Mobile optimization refers to the process of designing and developing websites, content, and marketing campaigns to be easily accessible and usable on mobile devices. It is important for a number of reasons:

Increased mobile usage: The number of people accessing the internet through mobile devices has increased dramatically in recent years, making it imperative for businesses to have a strong mobile presence.

Improved user experience: A mobile-optimized website provides a better user experience, with faster loading times and easy navigation, which can lead to increased engagement and conversions.

Better search engine rankings: Google and other search engines prioritize mobile-friendly websites in their search results, meaning a mobile-optimized site is more likely to rank higher and reach a larger audience.

Enhanced targeting: Mobile optimization allows businesses to better target and reach customers through location-based and context-sensitive advertising and marketing campaigns.

Increased conversions: Mobile-optimized websites and campaigns are more likely to convert visitors into customers, as they provide a seamless and optimized experience for mobile users.

Overall, mobile optimization is crucial for businesses to remain competitive in today's digital landscape, where mobile usage is prevalent and growing. By optimizing for mobile, businesses can reach and engage more customers, improve their search rankings, and drive increased conversions.

C. Mobile apps and mobile-friendly websites

Mobile apps and mobile-friendly websites are two key components of a comprehensive mobile marketing strategy.

Mobile apps are standalone software programs that can be downloaded and installed on a user's mobile device. They offer businesses the opportunity to provide a customized and engaging experience for customers, with features such as push notifications, in-app purchases, and offline functionality. Mobile apps can also collect valuable data and insights on customer behavior and preferences.

Mobile-friendly websites, on the other hand, are websites designed to be easily accessible and usable on mobile devices. They typically feature a responsive design that adapts to the size and orientation of the user's device, making it easier to navigate and interact with the site on a mobile device. Mobile-friendly websites also tend to load faster and offer a more streamlined user experience, making them more appealing to mobile users.

Both mobile apps and mobile-friendly websites have their unique advantages and can play a key role in a successful mobile marketing strategy. The choice between the two often depends on the business's goals and target audience, as well as the type of content and services they offer.

Overall, having a strong mobile presence through mobile apps and mobile-friendly websites is essential for businesses to reach and engage customers where they are most active and to drive increased conversions and engagement.

D. Measuring the success of mobile marketing

Measuring the success of mobile marketing involves tracking key metrics and performance indicators to determine the effectiveness of campaigns and strategies. Some common metrics used in mobile marketing include:

App installs and downloads: The number of users who have downloaded and installed a mobile app.

User engagement: The amount of time users spend within the app or on a mobile-friendly website.

Conversion rate: The number of users who complete a desired action, such as making a purchase or filling out a form.

Mobile traffic: The number of users accessing a website or app via a mobile device.

Push notifications open rate: The percentage of users who open push notifications sent from an app.

In-app purchases: The number of users who make a purchase within the app.

Bounce rate: The percentage of users who leave a website or app after only visiting one page.

Return on investment (ROI): A measure of the return generated from a marketing campaign, calculated as the revenue generated divided by the cost of the campaign.

By tracking and analyzing these metrics, businesses can gain insights into what is working well and what needs improvement, and make data-driven decisions to optimize their mobile marketing efforts. Regular monitoring and analysis of these metrics also helps businesses to stay ahead of changes in consumer behavior and technology trends, and to continually improve the effectiveness of their mobile marketing initiatives.

IX. Marketing Automation

Marketing automation refers to the use of software and technology to streamline, automate, and measure marketing tasks and workflows. The main objectives of marketing automation are to improve efficiency, increase effectiveness, and deliver a personalized customer experience.

With marketing automation, businesses can automate repetitive tasks such as email campaigns, social media posts, lead generation and nurturing, and analytics tracking. This allows marketing teams to focus on high-level strategic tasks, such as segmentation, personalization, and creative content development.

Marketing automation also enables businesses to collect and analyze customer data, including behaviors, preferences, and purchase history, to deliver a more targeted and personalized customer experience. This helps to build customer loyalty and increase customer lifetime value.

Key components of marketing automation include:

- Customer relationship management (CRM) software
- Lead management and nurturing tools
- Marketing analytics and reporting tools
- Email marketing and automation platforms
- Social media management and automation tools

By utilizing marketing automation, businesses can optimize their marketing efforts and achieve their goals, such as improving customer engagement, increasing conversions, and generating higher returns on investment.

A. Definition of marketing automation

Marketing automation refers to the use of software and technology to streamline, automate, and measure marketing tasks and workflows. The objective is to improve efficiency and effectiveness, and to deliver a more personalized customer experience. This includes automating repetitive tasks like email campaigns, social media posts, lead generation and nurturing, and analytics tracking. The use of marketing automation allows businesses to collect and analyze customer data to deliver a more targeted and personalized experience, build customer loyalty and increase customer lifetime value.

B. Benefits of marketing automation

Marketing automation offers several benefits to businesses, including:

Improved efficiency: By automating repetitive tasks, marketing teams can focus on high-level strategic tasks and make better use of their time.

Increased effectiveness: Marketing automation enables businesses to collect and analyze customer data to deliver a more targeted and personalized customer experience. This can lead to increased customer engagement and conversions.

Increased ROI: By automating and optimizing marketing processes, businesses can generate higher returns on investment from their marketing efforts.

Better customer experience: Marketing automation allows businesses to deliver a more personalized and consistent customer experience, which can increase customer loyalty and lifetime value.

Better data analysis: With marketing automation, businesses can collect and analyze customer data in real-time, allowing them to make informed decisions and adjust their marketing strategies as needed.

Improved lead management: Marketing automation helps businesses to track leads from initial contact to conversion, making it easier to identify and address any roadblocks in the sales process.

Increased scalability: With marketing automation, businesses can scale their marketing efforts without increasing headcount, making it easier to reach new customers and expand into new markets.

C. Choosing the right marketing automation tools

Choosing the right marketing automation tool for your business depends on several factors, including:

Business goals and objectives: Determine the specific goals you want to achieve through marketing automation, such as improving lead generation, increasing customer engagement, or improving the customer experience. This will help you choose a tool that is aligned with your goals.

Budget: Consider your budget and determine how much you are willing to spend on a marketing automation tool. Some tools can be expensive, while others offer a more affordable option.

Integration with existing systems: Make sure that the marketing automation tool you choose integrates with your existing systems, such as your CRM, email service provider, and website. This will ensure seamless integration and reduce manual effort.

User-friendliness: Choose a tool that is easy to use and navigate, and that has a user-friendly interface. This will reduce the learning curve for your team and increase adoption.

Data privacy and security: Consider the security measures in place for the marketing automation tool you choose. Make sure it has robust data privacy and security features to protect your customer data.

Customer support: Choose a tool that offers excellent customer support and has a strong reputation in the industry. This will ensure that you have access to help when you need it.

Customization options: Consider the customization options available with the marketing automation tool you choose. Make sure it can be tailored to meet your specific needs and requirements.

By considering these factors, you can choose a marketing automation tool that best fits your business and supports your marketing goals.

D. Measuring the success of marketing automation

Measuring the success of marketing automation is critical to determine its effectiveness and to make informed decisions about future campaigns. The following metrics are commonly used to measure the success of marketing automation:

Conversion rate: This measures the number of leads that convert into customers. This metric helps you determine the effectiveness of your campaigns in driving conversions.

Lead generation: This measures the number of new leads generated through marketing automation. This metric helps you determine the success of your lead generation efforts.

Open rate: This measures the number of emails that were opened and read by the recipient. This metric helps you determine the success of your email campaigns.

Click-through rate: This measures the number of clicks on links in your emails, social media posts, or other content. This metric helps you determine the effectiveness of your call-to-action.

Bounce rate: This measures the number of emails that were returned as undeliverable. This metric helps you identify any technical issues with your email campaigns.

Engagement rate: This measures the level of engagement with your content, such as likes, comments, shares, etc. This metric helps you determine the success of your content marketing efforts.

Return on investment (ROI): This measures the return on investment for your marketing automation campaigns, taking into account the cost of the campaign and the revenue generated. This metric helps you determine the financial success of your campaigns.

By regularly monitoring these metrics, you can gain insights into the performance of your marketing automation efforts and make data-driven decisions to improve your campaigns.

X. Conclusion

In conclusion, digital marketing plays a crucial role in today's business world, as more and more consumers are turning to the internet for information, products, and services. Understanding your target audience and creating a strong online presence through a well-designed website, effective social media use, and search engine optimization (SEO) is crucial. Utilizing different marketing strategies such as content marketing, email marketing, paid advertising, mobile marketing, and marketing automation can help businesses reach their desired target audience and drive conversions.

The success of each strategy can be measured through various metrics, such as conversion rate, open rate, click-through rate, engagement rate, and return on investment (ROI). By regularly monitoring these metrics, businesses can make data-driven decisions and continuously improve their digital marketing efforts.

A. Recap of key takeaways

Key Takeaways:

1. Digital marketing is crucial in today's business world as more consumers are turning to the internet.
2. Understanding the target audience and creating a strong online presence is essential to success.
3. A well-designed website, effective social media use, and SEO are important for building a strong online presence.
4. Content marketing, email marketing, paid advertising, mobile marketing, and marketing automation are various

strategies that businesses can use to reach their target audience and drive conversions.

5. The success of each strategy can be measured through various metrics, such as conversion rate, open rate, click-through rate, engagement rate, and return on investment (ROI).
6. Regular monitoring of these metrics can help businesses make data-driven decisions and continuously improve their digital marketing efforts.

B. Future trends in digital marketing

Some future trends in digital marketing include:

1. Artificial intelligence (AI) and machine learning (ML) are being integrated into various aspects of digital marketing to personalize customer experiences, analyze customer data, and automate routine tasks.
2. The use of chatbots and voice search optimization is increasing to provide customers with quick, convenient, and personalized assistance.
3. Video marketing is growing in popularity as more consumers prefer watching videos to reading text.
4. The importance of privacy and data security is increasing, and businesses are expected to prioritize these concerns when collecting and using customer data.
5. Interactive and immersive experiences such as augmented reality (AR) and virtual reality (VR) are becoming more prevalent in digital marketing.
6. Social commerce, where customers can make purchases directly through social media platforms, is becoming more widespread.
7. Influencer marketing is growing in popularity as consumers trust influencers more than traditional advertising.

8. Micro-moments, where consumers turn to the internet to quickly find information and make decisions, are becoming more important for businesses to address.
9. Personalized and omnichannel marketing, where businesses can reach customers across multiple devices and platforms, is becoming more important for success.

C. Final thoughts

In conclusion, digital marketing is a crucial aspect of modern business and is constantly evolving. To stay competitive, businesses need to continuously assess their digital marketing strategies, stay up-to-date with the latest trends, and make data-driven decisions. A strong online presence, effective content marketing, targeted email campaigns, and strategic use of paid advertising are just some of the many components of a successful digital marketing strategy. By understanding the needs and behaviors of the target audience, businesses can create targeted and effective campaigns that drive results and achieve their marketing objectives.

www.ingramcontent.com/pod-product-compliance
Lightning Source LLC
LaVergne TN
LVHW072052060326
832903LV00054B/405